SURREALISM

A clear insight into Artists and their Art

Pam Cutler

Barrington Stoke

Dedicated to Peter, Hannah and James for all their patience.

First published 2004 in Great Britain by
Barrington Stoke Ltd, Sandeman House, Trunk's Close,
55 High Street, Edinburgh, EH1 1SR

www.barringtonstoke.co.uk

Front cover image: The Lovers (1928) by René Magritte
Richard S. Zeisler Collection, New York, USA

ISBN 1-84299-180-9

Edited by Julia Rowlandson
Cover design by Helen Ferguson
Picture research by Kate MacPhee

Designed and typeset by GreenGate Publishing Services,
Tonbridge
Printed in Great Britain by The Bath Press

Barrington Stoke acknowledge support from the Scottish Arts
Council towards the publication of this title.

Scottish
Arts Council
LOTTERY FUNDED

Contents

Introduction

The actual meaning of the word Surrealism is beyond the real.

Surrealist artists wanted to find new ways of expressing themselves and a new approach to art. They painted strange dream-like pictures like Salvador Dalí's **The Persistence of Memory**, 1931. They changed real objects to make them appear strange like Meret Oppenheim's **Object for Breakfast**, 1936, in which the artist has covered the normally hard, smooth surfaces of a cup and saucer with animal fur.

Surrealists wanted to explore what went on beneath the surface of people's thoughts. They wanted to make people question their ideas about what was real.

In order to understand more about it we need to discover the answers to the following five questions:

- Where did Surrealism come from?
- What was Surrealism?
- Who were the Surrealists?
- What and who influenced Surrealist artists to work in the way they did?
- What were the methods artists used to create Surreal images?

PART ONE

Object for Breakfast (1936) by Meret Oppenheim
Museum of Modern Art (MoMA), New York, USA, © DACS 2004

Where did Surrealism come from?

Surrealism grew out of another art movement called Dada.

Dada began during the World War 1 (1914–1918) in a city called Zurich in Switzerland. Many artists, musicians and writers went there during the War because Switzerland did not join up with either side. These artists were horrified by the millions of people being killed and thought that it was a senseless waste of life. They also thought that it had all started because of the values held by society before the War and the greed of the people in charge.

They were fed up with politicians and everything that had supported the way of life before the War. They decided that the best way to put their point across was to challenge everything and they did this by poking fun at all the *traditions* that had been important before. So, they produced art objects from pieces of rubbish* and staged mad events which they said had no meaning at all. At a famous Dada exhibition held in Berlin in 1920, organised by **Max Ernst**, visitors were given axes so they could destroy any of the artworks if they wished! Writers wrote poems of complete nonsense and musicians made music of odd noises, played on kitchen pots and pans.

The Dada movement was a protest movement which had a lasting *influence*. It spread throughout Europe and was even taken up in New York by the artist, **Marcel Duchamp**, and his group. Dada showed artists that they could use just about anything in their work. It gave them the freedom to express themselves exactly as they wanted and have fun whilst shocking people by producing art which was *unconventional*. This means their work was not about *traditional* subjects and was often made using unusual materials.

* Kurt Schwitters' collages were made up of pieces of rubbish like bus tickets, cigarette packets, wallpaper and pieces of lace. This one is called Merz 318 CH., 1921.

tradition/traditional – a tried and tested way of doing things which is often handed down from one generation to another.

influence – something or someone which has affected the way an artist thinks or does something.

unconventional – if you are unconventional you do not follow the rules that most people agree with.

collage – an artwork made from cutting up other materials and pictures and sticking them together to make a new design.

Merz 318 CH., (1921) by Kurt Schwitters

Private Collection, © DACS 2004

However, by 1922, artists were becoming bored and fed up with Dada's negative approach and many of them began to explore the new ideas of Surrealism. This showed them the way to a new approach to art which still caused arguments but had more structure to its aims.

What was Surrealism?

Surrealism was at first a movement for writers

The ideas of Surrealism were first talked about by imaginative and poetic writers such as the French poets, **André Breton**, **Philippe Soupalt** and **Paul Eluard**.

One of the first Surrealist writings by André Breton was called *Les Champs Magnétiques* or *Magnetic Fields* which he published in 1919

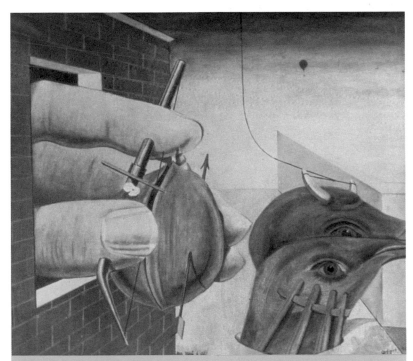

Oedipus Rex (1922) by Max Ernst is an early Surrealist work which uses techniques of collage and changes of scale.

Collection of Claude Herraint, Paris, France, © ADAGP, Paris and DACS, London 2004

How did they want to change things?

These poets wanted to challenge the *traditional* methods and content of writing. They tried to do this by experimenting with different ways of writing. They did not want to have *conscious* control over their own words or the subjects they wrote about.

In order to do this ...

- they recited and recorded their dreams
- they experimented with *automatic* writing.

Automatic writing was achieved by various methods such as:

- playing the children's game of consequences in which the writer continues a piece of writing without knowing what has been written just before
- by hypnotising themselves and writing down the things they said whilst in this state of mind
- by writing down unconnected words or sentences just as they popped into their head. There was no particular theme or purpose.

tradition/traditional – a tried and tested way of doing things which is often handed down from one generation to another.

conscious – relating to the reasoning part of the mind we use when we are awake and are aware that we are thinking.

automatic – a way of doing things without thinking about it and without conscious control.

The Secret Player (1927) by René Magritte
In this painting the Surrealist artist, René Magritte, has created a mysterious, dream-like image by putting disconnected things into a strange context.
Private Collection, © ADAGP, Paris and DACS, London 2004

Who were the Surrealists?

Who wrote the first Surrealist manifesto?

The poet, **André Breton** published the first Surrealist *manifesto* in 1924. In this he set out all his ideas and aims of Surrealism.

By this time there were lots of artists who wanted to express surrealist ideas through pictures and sculptures. Breton published a magazine called *The Surrealist Revolution* in which he wrote about and showed the work of Surrealist painters.

The main Surrealist artists working in the 1920s included:

Max Ernst	René Magritte
Joan Miró	Salvador Dalí
Yves Tanguy	Man Ray
André Masson	Jean Arp

Later, during the 1930s, many other artists expressed surrealist ideas in their work. These included:

Paul Nash	Oscar Dominguez
Frida Kahlo	Meret Oppenheim
Henry Moore	Leonora Carrington
Dorothea Tanning	Alberto Giacometti

Hope at 4am (1929) by Yves Tanguy
Musee National d'Art Moderne, Centre Pompidou, Paris, France, © ARS, NY

The Birthday (1942) by Dorothea Tanning
Philadelphia Museum of Art, Pennsylvania, PA, USA, © ADAGP, Paris and DACS, London 2004

What and who influenced Surrealist artists to work in the way they did?

The roots of Surrealism

Although the Surrealists said they were taking a brand new approach to art, this was not quite true. They admired many of the artists who had gone before, in particular the *Symbolists* and the Italian metaphysical painter **De Chirico**. They also took on the *revolutionary* ideas of the psychologist **Sigmund Freud** and the socialist writer **Karl Marx**.

Symbolist – the symbolist movement involved writers as well as artists. Symbolists were against realism in art and wanted to create pictures which were more imaginative and dream-like.

revolutionary – rebelling against what was generally accepted.

The Apparition (1876) by Gustave Moreau

Musee Gustave Moreau, Paris, France

The Scream (1895) by Edvard Munch

Nasjonalgalleriet, Oslo, Norway, © Munch Museum/Munch – Ellingsen Group, BONO, Oslo, DACS, London 2004

spiritual – the spiritual involves the inner, unworldly side of human understanding.

The influence of Symbolism

The *Symbolist* movement had its beginnings in the 19th century. Artists wanted to make paintings which were more meaningful and *spiritual*. They wanted to show what was going on in their imaginations.

- Some Symbolists illustrated myths and legends in their paintings in a new and sometimes shocking way, e.g. **Gustave Moreau's The Apparition**, 1876 (see page 10). This illustrated the bible story of Salome. It showed her having a vision of the chopped off head of St. John the Baptist.

- Others painted flat areas of unnatural colour and showed real and unreal scenes in the same painting, e.g. Paul **Gauguin's Vision after the Sermon**, 1888.

- Painters like Norwegian **Edvard Munch** stressed the more emotional side of their imagination in paintings such as **Dance of Life** of 1899 and **The Scream**, 1895 (see page 10).

- **Odilon Redon** created fantastic and mysterious images such as **The Eye like a Strange Balloon Mounts Towards Infinity**, 1882.

- **Arnold Böcklin**, a Swiss *Symbolist*, painted strange scenes to create different atmospheres such as **The Island of the Dead**, 1880. He said it was 'a picture for dreaming over'.

Although the Symbolists created images from their imagination in different and individual ways, they all tried to express an inner experience. It was this that attracted the Surrealists to them.

The Eye like a Strange Balloon Mounts Towards Infinity (1882) by Odilon Redon

Museum of Modern Art (MoMA), New York, USA

The Island of the Dead (1880) by Arnold Böcklin

Museum der Bildenden Kunste, Leipzig, Germany

The metaphysical painter, Giorgio De Chirico

The Surrealists were very much influenced by the early work of the Italian painter, **Giorgio De Chirico**. They loved the strangeness, the dream-like quality and uneasiness he achieved in his images. Many of the artists, including Magritte, Ernst and Dalí, used the ideas in De Chirico's paintings as starting points for their own work.

De Chirico, who was himself influenced by the Symbolist, Arnold Böcklin, created a series of paintings between 1910 and 1925 which he called *Metaphysical Painting*. He used this term to describe his work because he thought he was able to show a deeper reality behind the surface of the things he painted. By putting unlikely or odd objects next to each other, he said that he could open up their magical quality. For example, in his painting, **The Uncertainty of the Poet**, 1913 he creates an unsettling effect by putting a *classical* sculpture next to a bunch of bananas in an eerie, empty city landscape with long shadows.

De Chirico *distorted* space, painted shadows that were too long and put in strange collections of objects. He created dream-like pictures which disturb us and make us feel uneasy. The Surrealists really liked the way he could paint these strange scenes which made people feel so unsettled. His pictures were often called *enigmatic*.

The Uncertainty of the Poet (1913) by Giorgio De Chirico

metaphysics – the study of the true reasons why things exist and why we think.

classical – following the rules of art first established in ancient Greece and Rome.

distort – to twist or stretch something into a different shape, to deform it.

enigmatic – mysterious, uncanny, hard to understand.

The influence of the psychologist, Sigmund Freud

The *psychoanalyst*, Sigmund Freud, believed that dreams were the key to the *unconscious* mind. In 1900, he published his book *The Interpretation of Dreams* in which he describes processes which take place in our unconscious mind when we are dreaming. He said these processes were the way the mind finds a way round the *conscious* control of our thoughts and feelings, and shows us what our experiences really mean. He also used a method of 'free association' to help his patients. He would give them a word or idea and they would say the first thing they thought of. In this way Freud was able to find out how their minds worked.

Freud believed that when we develop adult reasoning, it hides the unconscious desires that we had when we were young. One of Freud's theories was called the Oedipus complex. He said we all go through this stage when we are very young. We identify totally with our mothers and do not see ourselves as separate individuals. We see the father as a threat to this bond with our mothers and want to replace him. These desires make us anxious and they are hidden in our *unconscious* minds. When we grow up they still affect all our thoughts and actions and influence the whole of society and culture. Freud found that he could help people with his method of psycho-analysis.

The Surrealists used Freud's theories and methods to inspire them in their creative lives. They did not want to explain the meanings of symbols in dreams but wanted to use their strange images as a powerful means to express themselves in their paintings.

When **Max Ernst** painted **Pietá Revolution by Night** in 1920, he was probably exploring Freud's theories about the *unconscious* feelings children have for their parents. It is an *enigmatic* painting in which Ernst shows himself as a boy lying on his father's lap. He is in the same position as the crucified Jesus often is, painted lying on his mother's lap. This is why Ernst gave it the title, **Pietá**.

Pietá Revolution by Night (1920) by Max Ernst
Penrose Collection, London, © ADAGP, Paris and DACS, London 2004

The influence of the socialist writer, Karl Marx

In the mid to late 19th century, **Karl Marx** wrote his thoughts on society and economy in his most famous series of books called *Das Kapital*. The ideas in these books inspired *Communism* and the Russian Revolution.

Surrealists agreed with the *Marxist* idea that society had to change. The Surrealists longed for a new view of the world which would bring about a big change in the way society was made up and the way things worked.

However, there was a clash between Freud's ideas on the importance of the individual and the Marxist political vision of everyone being equal. This lead to a tension within the aims of the Surrealism movement. In the end, it proved impossible to bring together the *spiritual* and emotional concerns of Freud with the *socio-economic* ideas of the *Communists*. It was because of this that **André Breton** and his colleagues were finally thrown out of the Communist Party in 1933.

enigmatic – mysterious, uncanny, hard to understand.

socio-economic – socio-economic theories involve the idea that all parts of people's lives are affected by the way things are made and distributed.

automatic/automatist –
a way of doing things without
thinking about it and without
conscious control.

What were the methods artists used to create surreal images?

The poet **André Breton** thought that if creative people were able to communicate directly with their *unconscious* minds they would release a huge amount of creativity. They could then make art which expressed experiences which lay beyond their *conscious* control. Visual artists responded to these ideas by using the same methods used by the poets and writers. They recited dreams and used *automatic* writing techniques (see page 8). The artists experimented with what they called *automatist techniques* which were based on effects happening by chance in their artwork. Others based their paintings on actual dreams they had experienced themselves.

Automatist techniques

André Masson and painting in gestures

- Produced fantastic and very colourful work. He put the paint onto the canvas in large brush strokes.
- Did not plan out his pictures but made unplanned gestures with his paintbrush.
- Forced himself into extreme states of mind by starving himself of food and sleep.
- Wanted to make works which linked directly with his passions and the impulses of his *unconscious* mind (**Sunrise at Montserrat**, 1935).

Sunrise at Montserrat (1935) by
André Masson
Galerie Daniel Malingue, Paris, France, © ADAGP,
Paris and DACS, London

Other artists experimented with finding images hidden in a piece of work which had been created by the artist without any planning. Chance and accident were seen as gateways into the world of the imagination.

Max Ernst and 'frottages'

- Made *'frottages'* which were made by taking rubbings from different surfaces. These were then put together and drawn over to create mysterious visions of fantastic worlds lived in by strange creatures, (**Forest and Dove**, 1927).

psychiatric – to do with the mind or mental disorders.

transformation/ transformed – changed from one form to another.

Oscar Dominguez and the ink-blot technique

- Dominguez took the ink-blot technique (used in *psychiatric* therapy to discover what was really going on in patients' minds) and adapted it to create extraordinary images. This way of working was described by the artist as *'decalcomanias* without preconceived aim'. In other words, the shapes found in random patches of ink were made sense of and developed into unusual *transformations* such as a lion turning into a bicycle (**Untitled Decalcomania**, 1936).

Untitled Decalcomania (1936) by Oscar Dominguez
Musee National d'Art Moderne, Centre Pompidou, Paris, France, © ADAGP, Paris and DACS, London 2004

Forest and Dove (1927) by Max Ernst
Tate, London, © ADAGP, Paris and DACS, London 2004

In *Dutch Interior* (1928), Joan Miró uses the technique of automatic drawing to create fantasy images from his unconscious mind.

Peggy Guggenheim Foundation, Venice, Italy, © Successio Miro, DACS, 2004

Man Ray, Yves Tanguy, Joan Miró and 'Exquisite corpses'

- The artists followed the poets' example and produced group works based on the children's game of Consequences. In this game each child draws a part of a body and folds the paper over. The players do not know what the whole drawing is like until they are shown it at the end. Likewise these artists produced drawings without knowing what their fellow artists had done until they saw the final drawing.

- Works produced in this way were called **Exquisite corpses** after a phrase made up in a game of Consequences played by the poets which came out as 'the exquisite corpse will drink the new wine'. Many of these drawings were published in André Breton's magazine called *La Révolution Surréaliste*.

Surrealists also made strange objects like Man Ray's *The Gift*, 1921. He has covered an iron, which we expect to be smooth, with spikes.

Private Collection

Dream paintings

René Magritte

The Belgian artist **René Magritte** (1898–1967) painted strange dream-like pictures in a style which made the objects and people in them look very *realistic*. He was excited by the paintings of **De Chirico**. He really liked paintings which showed everyday objects put together in an odd context. His ideas were also influenced by Freud's work on the processes of dreaming which he outlined in his book called *The Interpretation of Dreams*, published in 1900. In his paintings Magritte questioned the way we see the world and the links between the way we talk about things and our actual experience of the things themselves.

To show these ideas in his paintings Magritte used different methods

1. He altered the scale and proportion of everday objects and put them into strange contexts. He made rocks float, apples fill whole rooms and replaced people's faces with fruit or bunches of flowers (**The Listening Room**, 1958).

2. He showed objects changing themselves into something else such as the feet which become boots in **The Red Model** of 1937.

3. He often produced a sense of mystery by using symbols such as a jockey riding a horse to suggest a stressed, racing state of mind, or a train to suggest the passage of time. In **The Lost Jockey**, 1926 (see page 35), an anxious jockey searches in a mysterious forest of giant wooden spindles.

4. Magritte questioned whether we could be sure what we saw was actually there. In his painting called **The Human Condition**, 1930 (see page 40), he painted a beach scene in front of which stands an artist's easel. The painting on the easel is of the exact part of the landscape which would be behind it.

The Listening-Room (1958) by René Magritte
Menil Collection, Houston, TX, USA, © ADAGP, Paris and DACS, London 2004

The Red Model (1937) by René Magritte
Musee National d'Art Moderne, Centre Pompidou, Paris, France, © ADAGP, Paris and DACS, London 2004

realistic – true-to-life. A description of something which people agree is close to its appearance. In the past, Western artists have been expected to follow the rules of perspective and shading if they wanted to produce a picture which would be described as realistic.

The Betrayal of Images (1928–1929) by René Magritte
Los Angeles County Museum of Art, CA, USA, © ADAGP, Paris and DACS, London 2004

5. Magritte also made paintings about the difference between the words we use to describe the world we live in and the real things. The most famous of these is his painting of a pipe under which he wrote, '*Ceci n'est pas une pipe*' ('this is not a pipe'). In this painting which he called **The Betrayal of Images** of 1928–1929, Magritte points out that, although very *realistic*, this is only the image of a pipe not the real thing. He also mentions the random naming of objects – a Russian, for example, might have a very different word for this object. By this means Magritte questions the link between sound, word and object. For Magritte this rather weak link shows us how mysterious our thought processes are and how poetic our words can be.

Salvador Dalí

- The Spanish artist, **Salvador Dalí**, (1904–1989) also made dream paintings.

- He was fascinated by the research on dreams carried out by the psychanalyst **Sigmund Freud** and used many of the ideas from Freud's work in his paintings.

- He was very interested in Freud's ideas on states of *paranoia* in his patients. It seemed that this condition affected the way the patient became aware of things and worked out the meaning of what he, the patient, saw and experienced. This resulted in confusion between what was real and what was imagined. This idea haunted Dalí and he tried to bring about a similar state in his own mind in order to create his paintings. This way of working he called the paranoic critical activity.

- Using this method, he created fantasy scenes using a highly detailed painting technique which has been compared to a kind of hyper-real colour photography. His paintings resemble weird *hallucinations* in which objects change their form, e.g. clocks melt over the edges of boxes in **The Persistence of Memory**, 1931 (page 26); forms change from one object into another in **The Metamorphosis of Narcissus**, 1937 (page 30); and the shapes of things are *distorted* and can be read in different ways in **Spider of the Evening … Hope!**, 1940.

paranoia – a mental attitude where people distort and exaggerate their experiences.

hallucination – an hallucination is something you see and believe to be real but is, in fact, only in your imagination.

Biographies of Artists and their Paintings Explored

Salvador Dalí (1904–1989)

Paintings analysed:

The Persistence of Memory, 1931

Soft Construction with Boiled Beans –
Premonition of Civil War, 1936

Metamorphosis of Narcissus, 1937

René Magritte (1898–1967)

Paintings analysed:

The Threatened Assassin, 1926–1927

The Heart of the Matter, 1928

The Human Condition, 1935

Max Ernst (1891–1976)

Paintings analysed:

La Foresta Imbalsamata, 1933

Europe after the Rain, II, 1940–1942

Vox Angelica, 1943

PART
TWO

Self-Portrait with the Neck of Raphael (1920) by Salvador Dalí

Gala-Salvador Dali Foundation, Figueres, Spain, © Salvador Dali, Gala-Salvador Dali Foundation, DACS, London 2004

Born: 11th May 1904

Died: 23rd January 1989

Place of Birth: Figueras, in the Catalonia area of north-east Spain.

Family details: His father was a Government official. Dalí had one brother and one sister.

Paintings analysed:

The Persistence of Memory, 1931

Soft Construction with Boiled Beans – Premonition of Civil War, 1936

Metamorphosis of Narcissus, 1937

SALVADOR DALI

> *representation* – a way of showing how things look in an accurate and realistic way.

Childhood

Salvador Dalí's father was a Government official and his family were well-off. His elder brother died the year before Dalí was born and his sister, Ana Maria, was born 4 years later. Dalí started painting when he was a young boy and had his first exhibition in the theatre of his home town of Figueras in the Catalan part of Spain when he was only 14 years old.

Youth and self-portrait

Two years later when he was 16 he completed this self-portrait called **Self-Portrait with the Neck of Raphael**. He was then painting in an Impressionist style but, as the title suggests, he was already looking back to the work of the old masters. He particularly admired the *representational* paintings of the Spanish artist, **Velasquez**, and the Dutch painter, **Vermeer**.

Dalí was a student at the Madrid Academy of Fine Art between 1921 and 1923. However, he fell out with the teachers there because they were into modern trends and did not teach him about the painters of the past. He was finally expelled from the Academy for urging other students to demonstrate against the teaching staff.

Dalí's mother had died in 1921 which had made him deeply sad. In 1929, he painted a picture called **The Enigma of Desire – My Mother, My Mother, My Mother** in which he tried to show how very important she was to him. In this painting we see the typical kind of rock that can be found along Dalí's favourite part of the Spanish coastline. Dalí has changed the shape of the rock so it looks like a giant womb out of which his own head is being born. The most important things in Dalí's life at this time were his mother and the land he was born into, and in this painting Dalí has made them into one image.

The Enigma of Desire – My Mother, My Mother, My Mother (1929) by Salvador Dalí

Dali Staatsgalerie Moderner Kunst, Munich, Germany, © Salvador Dali, Gala-Salvador Dali Foundation, DACS, London 2004

Dalí and the Surrealists

In 1929 Dalí made a Surrealist film called *Un Chien Andalou* with his friend, the director **Luis Buñuel**. The film shocked audiences with images such as a girl's eye being slit by a razor.

Breton's Surrealist group in Paris was very impressed with the film Dalí and Buñuel had made and welcomed Dalí into the main group of Surrealist artists. In the summer of 1929, a group of these artists, including **René Magritte** and the poet **Paul Eluard**, visited Dalí in Spain.

Dalí fell in love with **Gala**, Paul Eluard's wife, and she became the inspiration for much of his art. From this point on, he worked hard to develop his painting technique and became very skilful in painting things so they looked real. He wanted to paint *distorted* dream *images* so they looked as real as photographs. He also began exhibiting in International Surrealist exhibitions and writing articles in magazines about the aims of Surrealist art.

Dalí married Gala in 1934 and in 1936 the Spanish Civil War broke out. He went on working but was deeply shocked by the War and painted some horrifying images. He exhibited paintings in the Surrealist exhibition in Paris in 1938 and also visited Sigmund Freud (see page 13), the *psychoanalyst*, whose writings and theories about human behaviour he admired.

distort – to twist or stretch something into a different shape, to deform it.

image – any mental picture.

psychoanalyst – one who studies behaviours of the mind.

anagram – a word or phrase made by rearranging the letters of another word.

Development of his career

In 1939 **Breton**, the leader of the Surrealists in Paris, expelled Dalí from the Surrealist group. Breton could not accept Dalí's fascination with **Hitler**, the German Nazi leader, and he didn't agree with Dalí's support of **Franco**, the Dictator of Spain. In 1940, Dalí and his wife decided to leave Europe and go to America where they lived until 1949. Breton gave Dalí the nickname '*Avida Dollars*' (meaning 'Greedy for Dollars') which was an *anagram* of Dalí's name.

mysticism – an understanding of hidden truths about the world, usually of a religious kind.

manifesto – to explain what they were trying to do artists wrote down their aims and often published these and called them their manifesto.

retrospective – a retrospective exhibition is one that looks back over an artists career and displays works completed over a long period.

Dalí continued to paint, write and sculpt and in 1942 *The Secret Life of Salvador Dalí* was published in America. Dalí was deeply shocked by the dropping of the atom bomb on the city of Hiroshima in Japan and became fascinated by *nuclear physics* and *mysticism*. He published his **Mystical** *Manifesto* in 1951. His paintings during this period often show subjects which explode into tiny pieces. The most well-known of these is based on a portrait of his wife called **Galatea of the Spheres**, 1952.

Dalí and his wife returned from America in 1949 and lived in Spain from then on. During the 1950s Dalí painted some large-scale religious subjects like the famous **Christ of St. John of the Cross**, 1951.

In 1964 there was a big exhibition in Tokyo looking back at Dalí's work, and in 1971 the **Salvador Dalí Museum** was opened in America. In 1974, Dalí set up the Musee Dalí in his home town of Figueras. He continued to exhibit all over the world and in 1979 there was another huge *retrospective* exhibition in Paris and London.

End of his career

In 1982 Dalí's wife, Gala, died and Dalí tried to commit suicide by refusing to drink. In 1984, he was badly burnt in a fire at his home. In 1989, he died of a heart attack and left all his money and artworks to the Spanish state.

Throughout his life, Dalí was a larger than life character who loved to shock and scandalise. He is probably the most well-known of the Surrealist artists and exhibitions of his work continue to attract a large number of visitors.

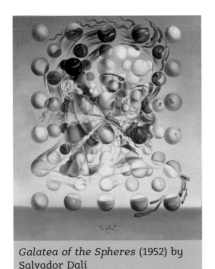

Galatea of the Spheres (1952) by Salvador Dalí

Gala-Salvador Dali Foundation, Figueres, Spain, © Salvador Dali, Gala-Salvador Dali Foundation, DACS, London 2004

The Persistence of Memory, 1931, by Salvador Dalí

Museum of Modern Art, New York, USA, © Salvador Dali, Gala-Salvador Dali Foundation, DACS, London 2004

Ideas:

- Experiment with changing the shapes of familiar objects. Look at their reflections in curved mirrors and draw how their shapes are stretched and *distorted*.

- Draw yourself asleep in an unusual place or environment. Add in some of the distorted shapes you have made.

- Try to recall some of your own dreams and put details of these in your paintings.

Background

Dalí loved the area of Spain where he was born. This was called Catalunya (Catalonia) and like many people from that region, Dalí had a great passion for food. He often put food in his paintings like pieces of bacon and beans. It is said that Dalí painted the melting watches in **The Persistence of Memory** because he had a dream about runny French cheeses!

Dalí also put striking images of real places in his pictures. The rocky landscape in this painting was probably based on the Catalan coastline that Dalí remembered from his childhood.

Another image that keeps coming up in Dalí's paintings is his own head. Its shape is stretched and *transformed* into a melting form.

distort/distortion – to twist or stretch something into a different shape, to deform it.

transformation/ transformed – changed from one form to another.

pun – a play on words that works by using a word which has two meanings.

hallucination – an hallucination is something you see and believe to be real but is, in fact, only in your imagination.

composition – the layout or formal design of a picture.

Content

This is a strange, fantasy landscape painted in a realistic way.

A bare tree grows out of a block of concrete and a watch hangs over one of its branches.

There are several watches in the picture. All of them have melted and are no longer made of the normal hard gold or silver. Dalí may be saying that in our dreams the passage of time is not the same as in our waking life. Time can be stretched and *distorted* or even stand still.

Dalí makes a kind of visual *pun* with the watch hanging on the tree. We often talk about time being 'suspended' and to suspend can mean to hang or to dangle.

The ants crawling over one of the watches may suggest things being eaten, or changing and decaying over the course of time.

The smooth rocky shape in the middle of the painting is Dalí's own head lying asleep with darkness all around it. You can recognise the shape of his nose and his eyebrows and lashes. His mouth is sealed which may mean that Dalí is dreaming and so cannot explain in words the things that he sees.

Form

Dalí described his paintings as hand-painted colour photography of images of *concrete irrationality*. What he meant was that he wanted to make the strange things from his dreams look so real that you would believe they existed. His paintings look like vivid *hallucinations*.

He uses blue and gold colours which give an unearthly feel to the scene. There is an eerie light and there are no signs of life on the distant clifftops.

All around Dalí's strange sleeping head is darkness. There is a similar *composition* in a painting that Dalí liked, called **The Island of the Dead**, 1880 (see page 11) by the Symbolist painter, Arnold Böcklin. Böcklin said it was a picture for dreaming over. In it there is a boat surrounded by darkness as it floats towards an eerily lit island.

Process

Dalí worked hard to improve his skills so that he could paint dream *images* which looked as real as photographs. He tried painting like the Impressionists and Cubists, but decided their pictures were not precise or *realistic* enough for him. He wanted to paint pictures from his dreams in a lot of detail so that strange things looked so real that we would believe they could exist.

Dalí admired the 'old masters' such as the Italian painter, Raphael. He also loved the realistic pictures of people at home by the Dutch artist, Vermeer.

Mood

This is a disturbing painting because it makes us question our ideas about real things. We find ourselves in a weird landscape where hard gold watches are turned into dripping formless shapes.

The whole scene in the painting looks weird and unearthly. It is lit by a strange light and Dalí's head lies sleeping by itself in the middle of the picture. His eyes are closed and his face has been stretched into an odd shape.

Soft Construction with Boiled Beans – Premonition of Civil War, 1936, by Salvador Dalí

Ideas:

- Try drawing *distortions* of the human face by looking at yourself in a curved or bendy mirror.

- Have you been to the hall of mirrors in a fairground or on a seaside pier? Try it out if you can and see what sort of images you come up with.

- Try drawing from different perspectives including the worm's eye viewpoint.

Background

Dalí completed this painting six months before the start of the Spanish Civil War, which he had predicted would happen. He said, '*The foreboding of civil war haunted me*'. Another painting called **Cannabilism in Autumn** was finished around this time and shows two people eating each other.

Dalí had always been obsessed with pictures of death and decay. When Europe was plunged into World War II, he painted horrific images such as **The Face of War**, 1940–1941, and **Spider of the Evening … Hope!**, 1940. He was asked to design props for a film called **Moontide** but they were so horrifying that the technicians refused to build them!

Dalí supported the *Fascists* and Franco during the war. The other Surrealists did not agree with this because most of them were *Communists* and believed in the ideas of Karl Marx (see page 14). In 1939, Breton finally threw Dalí out of the Surrealist group because he did not like Dalí's fascination with Hitler, leader of the Nazi party in Germany.

foreboding – threatening.

distort/distortion – to twist or stretch something into a different shape, to deform it.

grotesque – something which looks very odd and unnatural, often exaggerated, deformed and ugly.

Salvador Dalí – Soft Construction with Boiled Beans – Premonition of Civil War, 1936

Content

This horrific image shows a monstrous human body tearing itself apart.

The body rises up from a barren Spanish landscape and is meant to represent Spain and its people being torn apart by Civil War.

The body's mutilated parts lay all around on the ground. It is screaming with pain as it dies.

The body is propped up on a cupboard with drawers. Dalí painted drawers in many of his paintings and they were meant to be where we keep all the secrets from the unconscious mind.

Dalí often put food in his pictures and here he has sprinkled around pieces of meat and boiled beans. It makes you think of soft things inside the body like the liver and heart.

Form

This picture is drawn from below and we look up at the screaming face. This unusual viewpoint exaggerates the pain and agony in the face and the *distorted* body.

The arms and legs are stretched to breaking point and the head and shoulders look like a *grotesque* monster against the sky.

Process

Dalí planned the drawing in this picture so that it would have the most dramatic and *grotesque* effect. We stare up into the face which grimaces in agony against a powerful sky.

The shapes of the human body are stretched and *distorted*. The size of the hands and feet are larger-than-life and the muscles in the arms and neck stand out.

Mood

The mood of this painting is deeply disturbing.

Dalí's horrifying vision of civil war is sickening and painful to look at.

The stretched and torn human body parts are gruesome. The bits of food scattered over the body are horrifying.

The image is shocking and violent and has a very strong effect which you cannot forget.

Metamorphosis of Narcissus, 1937, by Salvador Dalí

Tate, London, © Salvador Dali, Gala-Salvador Dali Foundation, DACS, London 2004

Ideas:

- Try looking at other myths in a similar way. The myth of Pygmalion would be an interesting one to research. Can you think of any others?

- Study reflections in water. See how your own reflection is distorted in the surface of the water. Try drawing and painting what you see.

- Do a piece of work on the theme of vanity, which is when someone is too proud of their looks or abilities. This could be a *collage* of collected pictures from magazines, faces of celebrities, etc.

Background

Of all the Surrealist artists, Salvador Dalí was the one who was most fascinated by the ideas of the *psychoanalyst*, Sigmund Freud. In fact, Dalí met Freud in London in 1938, and took his painting called **Metamorphosis of Narcissus**, 1937, along to show him.

Freud had written about different types of personality disorders and states of mind. One of these was the *narcissus* type which was when a person is obsessed with himself.

Freud agreed that Dalí had succeeded in painting images from his unconscious mind but he thought Dalí's pictures were too obvious. He preferred pictures where he could discover for himself the workings of an artist's unconscious mind hidden within the work.

psychoanalyst – someone who studies behaviours of the mind.

narcissism – an excessive love of oneself.

paranoia – a mental attitude where people distort and exaggerate their experiences.

hallucination – an hallucination is something you see and believe to be real but is, in fact, only in your imagination.

ominous – something that is strange and threatening and may be a warning of bad luck to come or an evil thing about to happen.

Content

This painting is based on a Greek *myth*. Narcissus was a youth who fell madly in love with his own reflection in a pool. He thought it was a beautiful nymph or spirit that lived in the water there. He tried to reach the lovely nymph but of course he couldn't. In the end he gave up hope and killed himself. From his blood grew a delicate flower which was named after him and called a Narcissus.

You can see the two rocks at the edge of the pool as double images. One of them looks like a youth staring into the pool and the other like a hand holding an egg out of which the Narcissus flower is growing.

In the background Dalí shows a *mythical* landscape in which strange beasts prowl around. A group of nymphs dance in a stream behind the young man but Narcissus is too interested in his own reflection to notice them.

On the right-hand side of the painting there is a sculpture of a youth standing on a pedestal. This is probably meant to be Narcissus.

Form

A fiery, orange glow lights up the landscape. This produces an unreal atmosphere.

There are dark storm clouds which create a threatening mood. There is only one patch of blue sky above the mountains. A monstrous giant is silhouetted against the blue sky.

Dalí has painted a powerful, rocky landscape in dark reds and browns. It looks as though it is in ancient times because there are few signs of civilization. There is only one building in the distance. It is a strange landscape where myths and miracles might happen.

In the *foreground* of the painting there is a large figure of the young man, Narcissus. He is sitting gazing at himself in the water. Next to him is a stone hand, the same size and in the same position. The finger and thumb hold a stone egg out of which grows the narcissus flower.

The whole painting is like one big reflection. The blue of the sky and the rocky mountains are reflected in the pool. The body of the young man is reflected by the stone hand.

Process

Dalí called his method of creating double images in his paintings the **paranoiac-critical method**. The state of mind called *paranoia* had been researched by the psychoanalyst Sigmund Freud. He had discovered that patients suffering from the state of paranoia would have *hallucinations* which confused things that were real with those that were imagined.

Dalí got himself into a similar state of mind on purpose. In this way he was able to record what might be called 'visual hallucinations' or double images where one thing turns into another.

A good example of this can be seen in his painting called **Slave Market with Disappearing Bust of Voltaire**, 1940. The head of the famous French writer, Voltaire, can also be seen as a group of people.

Mood

The *ominous* lighting and unearthly landscape in this painting make us believe that something unexplainable and magical is taking place.

The pool where Narcissus sits admiring his reflection is completely still and there is an atmosphere of unnatural silence. The youth's body changes in a mysterious way. Sometimes it looks like it is made out of flesh and other times it looks like stone.

The dancing nymphs and odd creatures which live in this land make it a strange place where timeless myths can happen.

René Magritte behind the glass door of his house in Brussels, April 1967.

Born: 21st November 1898
Died: 15th August 1967
Place of birth: Lessines in Belgium
Family details: Magritte was the eldest son of three boys. His father was a tailor and merchant and his mother made hats.
Paintings analysed:
The Threatened Assassin, 1926–1927
The Heart of the Matter, 1928
The Human Condition, 1935

RENÉ MAGRITTE

Self-portrait

In his self-portrait called **Perspicacity**, 1936, Magritte showed himself working at his easel. His aim in painting was to show the processes of thought that the artist went through when he was working. In his own work, he was really fascinated by objects and their relationship to each other. In this painting, whilst he studies the egg on the table in front of him, he is actually making a painting of what he knows the egg will eventually turn into – a bird in flight.

Childhood

Magritte was born in Lessines, Belgium and was the eldest of three boys. His father was a tailor and merchant and his mother was a milliner. Although the family was middle class, they were not rich. When René was young, the Magritte family moved around a lot in order to improve their business.

Youth

A tragic event overtook the family in 1912. Magritte's mother suffered from depression and, when René was only fourteen years old, she committed suicide. She drowned herself in the River Sambre in Chatelet and was found with her nightgown wrapped around her face.

In 1916, Magritte became an art student at the **Academy of Fine Arts in Brussels**. Between 1918 and 1920, he produced paintings in a cubist style, he illustrated poems and he designed posters and advertisements.

Magritte and the Surrealists

In 1922, Magritte married Georgette Berger who he often used as his model in his paintings. He was also introduced to the work of the Italian painter, **Giorgio De Chirico**, and was very impressed.

In 1925, he made a contract with a gallery called La Centaure in Brussels. He painted a lot at this time and completed about 60 paintings a year. In 1927, he had his first one-man exhibition in the gallery and exhibited many of his early Surrealist paintings, including **The Lost Jockey**.

The Lost Jockey (1926) by René Magritte
Private Collection, © ADAGP, Paris and DACS, London 2004

Magritte and his wife went to Paris and took part in the activities of the Surrealists there. He made friends with **André Breton** and **Paul Eluard** (whose wife later married Dalí) and put work into the first group exhibition by the Surrealists in Paris.

He became one of the main figures in the Surrealist group in Paris and in 1929, published an article called 'Words and Images' in the magazine *La Revolution Surrealiste*. However, in 1930, he quarrelled with Breton (who was a fanatic anti-Catholic) and both Magritte and his wife returned to Belgium. They lived in the capital city of Brussels and met often with a group of Surrealist artists there.

Development of his Career

Throughout his life Magritte exhibited in Brussels, New York, Paris, London and Rome. He contributed to many magazines and illustrated poems. He also completed wall paintings and sculptures.

In 1965, **The Museum of Modern Art** in New York arranged a large exhibition looking back at Magritte's work. In 1967, there were also big exhibitions in Rotterdam and Stockholm. Magritte died in August of the same year (1967). Since then his paintings have been enjoyed by many people.

The Threatened Assassin, 1926–1927, by René Magritte

Museum of Modern Art (MoMA), New York, USA, © ADAGP, Paris and DACS, London 2004

Ideas:
- Have you read any novels or seen any films which have deeply affected you? If so, use them as a source of inspiration to create your own mysterious scene where a bizarre or horrifying event has just taken place. Try to create a sense of mystery and make the viewer of your painting wonder what is going to happen next.

- Try to create a painting of mixed emotions in which the expression on the main person's face does not match the content of the picture.

Background

The idea probably came from the 32 stories about Fantômas, a criminal genius, written by Pierre Souvestre and Marcel Allain between 1911 and 1914 and later made into films.

The stories were different from most thrillers, as the hero was the evil criminal, Fantômas, who brought bad luck to everyone around him. He was an expert in disguise and always avoided being caught. Fantômas stood for the darker side of human nature which was hidden in the unconscious and had no respect for society's laws.

Fantômas was like another character called Maldoror. Maldoror appeared in a book called *Les Chants de Maldoror* written by the poet, Lautreamont. The Surrealists loved the way this writer linked objects and ideas in *absurd* and strange ways. One of his most famous phrases was '*as beautiful as ... the fortuitous encounter upon an operating-table of a sewing machine and an umbrella.*"

The Surrealists took on Fantômas and Maldoror as their heroes as they wanted to shock and mystify people. **The Threatened Assassin**, 1926–1927, looks like something which might happen in one of the Fantômas stories.

absurd – a word used to describe something which is out of place and doesn't make sense. It is usually impossible to explain.

Content

This picture is set up like a scene from a film. You feel something dramatic is just about to happen. Perhaps, the identical men waiting outside will rush in and surprise the man in the room in some horrible act. The only difference between them is that one holds a weapon, which looks like part of a human arm, and the other holds a net. They could be detectives.

Inside the room, a woman lies dead on the bed, with blood running out of her mouth. The man with her seems to be in a world of his own, listening to music. He is a mysterious figure and you wonder what he has done or is about to do. His case lies on the floor possibly with disguises in it or the means of his escape. This man could be like the character of Fantômas.

There are no real clues as to what is going on. It is like a mind game in which you make up your own story about what is taking place.

Form

Magritte has put a lot of thought into the way his painting is arranged. There are two walls on either side at the front which make the picture very *symmetrical*. The lines on the floor make you look through the room to the window in the far wall.

Magritte is setting a scene as though it is on a theatre stage. The two identical men in bowler hats at the front look like they are hiding behind a stage curtain. He has put all the objects and people in exact positions as though they are ready to act on stage.

Outside the window, three men who look exactly the same, are watching the scene in silence. They do not react and show no signs of feeling or emotion. Behind them there is a strange landscape of bare mountains.

Process

Magritte worked in oil paint but you cannot see any brushstrokes in his paintings. Magritte said that it would make no difference if his paintings were made into posters because the ideas in them were the most important thing not the way he used the paint. This made some people think his style was too intellectual.

The way Magritte paints does in fact support his ideas. The shadows are menacing and the lack of brushstrokes and texture creates a sense of stillness and suspense.

This picture is not very colourful. Magritte uses a lot of black and his other colours are dull greys and browns. The couch on which the dead woman is lying stands out a lot because of its lurid red colour.

Mood

This painting has a disturbing effect. It creates a sense of mystery and suspense. You wonder what horrible thing has taken place and what is going to happen next.

Magritte repeats the same kinds of figures in his paintings. He paints men in suits and bowler hats who have identical faces. This makes them look *anonymous* and without individual characters. It also makes them look sinister and disturbing because they watch in silence and show no emotion.

It is unsettling to see how the 'assassin' is not affected by the terrible crime that has taken place. The event seems frozen in time. The people have stopped still in their positions and so we will never know what happens in the end.

The Heart of the Matter, 1928, by René Magritte

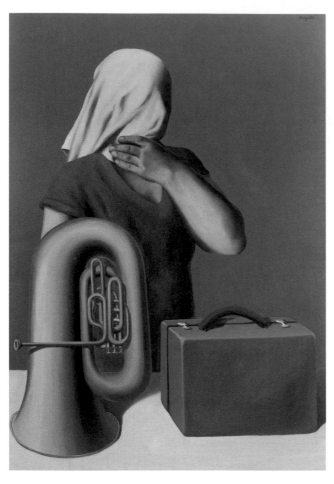

Background

Around the same time as Magritte was painting **The Threatened Assassin**, he made a series of strange paintings of people with their faces hidden. Some of these paintings share the same title – **The Lovers** (see front cover) and show a man and a woman with their heads covered by cloths. Their identities are hidden from each other and this stops any real contact between them. One of the most intriguing paintings from this period is called **The Heart of the Matter**.

Ideas:

- Collect together some things which had meaning to you from past periods of your life. Try to choose objects which are familiar to you but look very different from each other. Arrange them on a table against a plain background and make drawings and a painting from them.

- Magritte used other methods of making us look at familiar objects in a new and fresh way. Sometimes he changed the size of things as in the painting called **The Listening Room**, 1958 (see page 18) where the apple is so huge that it fills the whole room. He also put unexpected objects into his work as **In The Battle of the Argonne**, 1959, where a rock floats in the sky instead of a cloud. Try out these ways of working for yourself. Change the way we look at things by changing their size and scale or putting them in unexpected places.

ambiguity – an expression which has more than one meaning and this makes it unclear. Often completely different conclusions can be reached depending on which meaning is taken.

incongruous – not belonging to the place it is in.

Content

In **The Heart of the Matter** a woman is standing behind a table on which she has put a trombone and a case. The things in the painting seem *absurd* because they have nothing to do with each other. This creates a feeling of strangeness and mystery.

Magritte was fascinated by what he called 'the mystery of objects'. He could remember, when he was only a little baby, staring at a crate somebody had left beside his cradle.

Magritte painted the same objects in many of his paintings. There is a case on the floor in **The Threatened Assassin**. It is probably full of disguises to help the criminal, Fantômas, escape. Fantômas usually disguised himself by putting a stocking or cloth over his head like the woman in this painting.

However, some people think that the woman in **The Heart of the Matter** could refer to Magritte's unconscious memory of his mother who committed suicide by drowning herself when he was 14 years old. She was found with her nightgown wrapped around her face.

Form

The background of this painting is very plain so it makes you concentrate on the objects and the woman. Everything is painted to look 3-dimensional and *realistic*. The trombone and case stand out in the foreground which makes them look special and mysterious.

There is a mystery about the identity of the woman. Not only is her face covered but her hand looks very masculine. This is confusing and makes you wonder whether the person is male or female.

What is the meaning of the hand gesture? Is the hand holding down the veil or grasping the woman's throat? This painting may be linked to another one painted around the same time called **Gigantic Days**, 1928. In this painting a man and woman struggle with each other but they share the same body. Magritte was interested in the ideas about sexual desire and human behaviour which had been researched by the *psychoanalyst*, Sigmund Freud in his book *The Interpretation of Dreams*.

Process

The objects have clear outlines and there is no *ambiguity* about the space each one occupies. They are separate and this exaggerates the particular qualities of each one.

You are unaware of the media of oil paint being used because there are no visible brushstrokes or textural marks. The background is plain and there are no distractions from the main subject of the painting. The image is clear and *unambiguous* and this reflects the clarity of thought of the artist.

Mood

The arrangement of the veiled figure with these *incongruous* objects, that look strange when put in the same picture, is very disturbing. The image creates an unsettling feeling in the viewer.

The colours and tones are sombre and produce a mood of foreboding and loneliness.

Magritte loved the work of the Italian painter, Giorgio de Chirico. He painted incongruous objects next to each other in strange surroundings. In De Chirico's **The Uncertainty of the Poet**, 1913 (see page 12) a sculpture of a headless female torso stands next to a bunch of bananas. They are both put in an odd setting of old classical arches with a train rushing past in the distance. This painting creates an effect of strangeness and mystery similar to that of **The Heart of the Matter**.

The Human Condition, 1935, by René Magritte

Ideas:

- Paint a scene like this one, which is partly a real landscape and partly a painted image on an artist's easel. Play around with these trick effects. Things from the real landscape can pass through your painted version. For example, you can paint a flock of birds flying across the sky, through your canvas, and out the other side.

- Using Magritte's idea, you can paint a scene somewhere else. You could draw a corner of your bedroom in a picture on an easel and the rest of the room behind. The two parts of your picture should join up exactly.

Background

Magritte was fascinated by how we try to understand theworld around us by attaching words and pictures to it. However, he questioned the power of art and language to communicate clearly, without confusions.

Why should an apple be called an apple and not another name? Painting was often concerned with copying the appearance of things but no matter how well the artist painted it, it was still only a picture not the real thing.

He said that he was involved more in the process of thinking than that of painting. Many of his paintings are mind puzzles. Magritte believed that objects were very mysterious. He challenged how we see everyday things by painting the unexpected and making rocks float, apples hide faces, trombones burst into flames and roses fill whole rooms!

One of the most well known of his paintings about human *perception* (how we see things) was called **The Human Condition**, 1935.

randomly – something done randomly means that the outcome of the action is left to chance, for example, tossing a coin.

40

Content

In this picture there is an easel with a painting of a beach scene on it. Through the arched doorway you can see exactly the same beach in the distance.

The painting fits perfectly into the real scene behind as though it is part of it. We only know it is a painting because we can see the edge of the canvas and it is clearly in front of the wall.

Magritte is playing around with ideas about what is real and what is not. The easel and the black ball on the floor have been carefully drawn and painted with shadows to make them look real and 3-dimensional. The nail sticking out of the top of the easel looks very real too.

The main idea that Magritte is trying to put across is that, even though the painting is so like the real beach scene, it is still just a picture of it. This is what Magritte thought was the 'human condition'. We always have to make sense of our experiences by using the language of words, painting, and so on but we can never be sure how close we are to the truth.

Form

Magritte has used mainly cool colours.

The objects have clear and precise edges and outlines.

The *composition* is very exact and Magritte has measured everything out mathematically. The ball on the floor is a perfect sphere.

The easel looks very clean and new. It is not a working artist's easel. There are no tubes of paint, messy patches of paint or brushes. This easel is perfect.

The sea is very calm and stretches away into the distance.

Process

Although this is an oil painting, there is little texture and there are mainly flat areas of colour.

There are no patches of bright colour to focus on. The sea is painted in the same flat way until it reaches the horizon. There are no boats to distract the viewer.

The composition is precisely drawn out. It is a construction of the artist's imagination and not a real scene.

Mood

Although there is a suggestion of waves, this is a calm flat sea. You can imagine there is hardly a sound when the waves reach the shore. The horizon seems a long way off and everything seems frozen in one moment of time.

This painting makes you want to sit and think because everything is so still and perfect.

The Meeting of Friends (1922) by
Max Ernst

Ludwig Museum, Cologne, Germany, © ADAGP,
Paris and DACS, London 2004

Born: 2nd April 1891
Died: 1st April 1976
Place of birth: Bruhl in Germany
Family details: His father was a teacher of deaf
children. Ernst was one of seven children.
Paintings analysed:
La Foresta Imbalsamata, 1933
Europe after the Rain, II, 1940–1942
Vox Angelica, 1943

MAX ERNST

controversial – causing argument or difference of opinion.

decalcomania – a way of creating a texture in paint which can then be worked into to create different images.

frottage – a process of making rubbings from different surfaces such a floorboards, bark of trees, leaves, etc.

grattage – a technique of scraping away paint layers to show the canvas or other layers of dried paint beneath.

fascist/fascism – is an extreme nationalist movement. Fascists often believe that people's ideas and actions are a result of their race. They are opposed to the idea that people can solve their problems using reason. Fascist organisations usually have one strong leader.

Childhood

Max Ernst was born near the city of Cologne in Germany, in 1891. His father was a teacher of the deaf and he was also an accomplished painter. Max Ernst was the first son of a family of seven children and was born a year after the tragic death of his 6-year-old sister.

Youth

When he was 18, Ernst began studying philosophy, psychiatry and art history at Bonn University. Ernst was fascinated by the artwork produced by mental patients and was interested in new ways of expressing mood and emotion.

In 1911, he met the Expressionist painter, **August Macke**, and a year later he was influenced by a large exhibition in Cologne of International modern painters.

In 1914, when he was 23, he was called up to serve in the Armed Forces during World War I. He was deeply affected by his experiences and after it, disgusted with the horror of war, he became an important member of the **Cologne Dadaist Group**. He took part in a *controversial* exhibition of Dadaist art in Cologne in 1920 which the Authorities closed down.

Ernst used techniques of *decalcomania*, *frottage* and *grattage* to create disturbing images like **The Horde**, 1927. In this picture, wild men and scary creatures with claws fight their way out of the forest. Some people have seen this work as looking ahead to the rise of *Fascism* in Europe and the violence which was to come in World War II.

The Horde (1927) by Max Ernst
Stedelijk Museum, Amsterdam, © ADAGP, Paris and DACS, London 2004

Ernst and the Surrealists

In 1921, the poet and co-founder of the Paris Surrealist movement, **Paul Eluard**, visited Ernst in Cologne. At this time, Ernst was producing his own Surrealist dream paintings such as **The Elephant of the Celebes**. However, he was so impressed with Eluard and his wife, Gala, (who later married Dalí) that he left everything behind in Germany and went to live with them in Paris in 1922.

Self-portrait

The Elephant of Celebes (1921) by Max Ernst

Tate, London, © ADAGP, Paris and DACS, London 2004

In the same year, 1922, Ernst painted the group portrait called **The Meeting of Friends** (see page 42) which brings together many of the founders of Surrealism. Ernst is dressed in a green suit and sits on the left of the front row. The writers and artists communicate with each other in the sign language of the deaf which Ernst had seen used by the pupils in his father's school. André Breton, the main founder of the Surrealist movement, is shown as a dramatic figure in a red cloak. Behind him stands de Chirico, the Italian painter who influenced so many Surrealist artists (see page 12).

Of all the Surrealist artists, Ernst was the most *innovative* in exploring new and unexpected techniques. He liked using painting and drawing methods which relied mostly on chance effects and randomly created textures. Throughout the years 1925 to 1939 he published collections of his *collages* and *frottages*.

He was well-known in Surrealist groups, and in 1930 he acted in an outstanding Surrealist film directed by Luis Buñuel called *L'Age d'Or* or *The Golden Age*. During this time he also took part in major exhibitions in Paris and New York, showing his series of paintings on forests as well as fantasy landscapes using the *grattage* (scraping) and *decalcomania* (producing textures by lifting paint off the surface of the canvas) techniques.

innovative – to be innovative is to make changes to the old way of doing things or to do things in a new way.

Alchemy (1947) by Jackson Pollock
Peggy Guggenheim Foundation, Venice, Italy,
© ARS, NY and DACS, London 2004

Development of his career in America

In 1941, he fled from Europe and arrived in New York. He met and married the artist, **Dorothea Tanning** and developed a new series of paintings using the drip technique and geometric designs. He influenced many of the younger American artists such as **Jackson Pollock** in producing action painting and Abstract Expressionist works.

Return to Europe and the final years of Ernst's career

Ernst returned to Europe in 1950 and had an exhibition of his work in his home town of Bruhl in Germany in 1951. He continued to work producing plaster and bronze sculptures as well as paintings. The Tate Gallery in London had a big *retrospective* exhibition in 1962, and there were other large exhibitions of his work in 1969 and 1970 in Stockholm, Amsterdam and Stuttgart.

Max Ernst died in Paris on 1st April, 1976, one day before his 85th birthday.

retrospective – a retrospective exhibition is one that looks back over an artist's career and displays works completed over a long period.

La Foresta Imbalsamata, 1933, by Max Ernst

Ideas:

■ Try Ernst's techniques of **frottage** (rubbing) and **grattage** (scraping). You can make rubbings of floorboards, the barks of trees, leaves, etc. and then see whether you can find images from your own imagination hidden within the marks you have made.

■ Build up layers of paint and then scratch through the top layers to show the colours beneath. You can create textures in this way or use it as a method of drawing and create pictures from your imagination.

Background

Max Ernst wanted to create particular moods or feelings in his work but he was not interested in using *traditional* methods of painting. He wanted to experiment with different and less controlled ways of using paint and liked the fact that chance played a large part in how he produced his pictures. His methods were described as *automatist* because he tried to make his paintings without thinking too much beforehand. Ernst thought they were a way of getting past his *rational* thoughts and into the imaginative world of his *unconscious* feelings and desires.

La Foresta Imbalsamata is one of a series of pictures of forests. Paintings such as **Fishbone Forest**, 1927, have the same wall of trees and strange circular object looming in the sky. Ernst was fascinated by forests and spoke of the '*enchantment and terror*' he had felt as a young child when his father took him into woods for the first time.

tradition/traditional – a tried and tested way of doing things which is often handed down from one generation to another.

automatic/automatist – a way of doing things without thinking about it and without conscious control.

rational – using sense, reason or logic.

unconscious – the part of our minds that we usually only become aware of in our dreams and not when we are awake and using our powers of reason.

foreboding – threatening.

Content

A thick forest of tall, dark trees spreads across the picture. The trees grow very close together and you can hardly see through them. The forest could represent the tangled feelings and desires that fill our *unconscious* mind.

On the far side of the trees you can just see a mysterious, silvery ring floating in the sky. We are not sure what it means or why it is there. This circular form could be a symbol of the desire for unity in the mind of the artist. On the other hand, it may be more sinister and represent a strange, unknown world rising above the forest.

Ernst has drawn a bird in white dots across the front of the forest. This is probably a version of the bird who Ernst named 'Loplop, Bird Superior'. This bird represented the artist himself and it could move freely between the real world and that of the imagination.

Birds played an important role in Ernst's work. He used them as *symbols* for mankind as well as to represent himself. One of Ernst's friends described him as a bird of prey and wrote, '*Max Ernst has departed alone for the woods that no hunter has ever seen*'.

Form

The shapes of trees are painted in dark greens and browns. They are formed by the process of *frottage* and *grattage*. The scraped marks on the tree trunks make the trees look more solid and threatening.

The tops of the trees are twisted together and are almost impossible to get through.

In contrast, the delicately drawn bird-creature is transparent. It seems to pass through the forest with ease and is able to penetrate its darkness.

Process

In this painting Ernst combined the techniques of *frottage* and *grattage*.

The technique of frottage enabled the artist to create impressions of things like tree bark, floorboards, etc. He then worked into the marks to create fantastic textures and images. These rubbings form the basis of the rich texture of the forest.

Ernst has also used the technique of grattage where he has scraped away at the layers of paint to reveal the colours of dried paint beneath. This again creates a highly textured surface.

Mood

The painting has a sombre mood. The bird's outline shape is fragile against the dark forest. The dimly lit sky has a feeling of *foreboding*. It is unclear whether the glowing circle is rising or sinking in the sky of this strange world.

Ernst's forests are dark, disturbing places. There is no way of telling what horrors hide inside them. There was only one painting in the forest series which shows wild, aggressive creatures forcing their way out of the woods. It is called **The Horde** (see page 43) and was painted in 1927. Some people have seen this work as looking ahead to the violence of the Fascist movement and World War II.

Europe after the Rain, II, 1940–1942, by Max Ernst

Background

The years leading up to World War II were difficult ones for Max Ernst. He was horrified by the Spanish Civil War and wanted to fight on the *Republican* side. He was very upset when they were defeated by the *Fascists* and their leader, Franco.

The Fascist Nazi party in Germany had helped Franco in Spain. The Nazis now wanted to spread their power throughout Europe and they started taking over other countries. German troops invaded France in 1940.

In Germany, the Nazis destroyed work by artists who they didn't like and took some of Ernst's paintings out of art galleries. These paintings were never seen again. Ernst was arrested and put in prison several times between 1939 and 1941 but managed to escape from France and flee to America in 1941.

Before Ernst left for New York he began **Europe after the Rain** which showed a shocking landscape torn apart by war. Ernst sent the canvas ahead to the Museum of Modern Art in New York and collected it when he arrived. He went on working on it in America until 1942 which is why it is called **Europe after the Rain**, II.

Ideas:

- Try out the *decalcomania* technique yourself. Spread paint thickly onto a surface such as a polystyrene sheet or piece of lino. These sheets can be cut into any shape you like. When they are painted, press them down onto your paper and then pull them off. It's the same process as taking a print but you use acrylic or oil paints and not printing ink. When you have created a rich texture using this method, focus your mind on the shapes you can see in it and let your imagination run wild.

- When you have experimented with Ernst's techniques, try building up your own strange landscape.

Content

Europe after the Rain, II shows a horrific war-torn landscape. It foretells the devastation and terrible loss of life which was to come about in World War II.

Ernst made this painting just before he fled from Europe to America in 1941. German troops had overrun many countries in Europe and the Nazis were smashing everything in their path. The European way of life was being destroyed.

There are no buildings or features you can recognise in this landscape. The whole landscape has been overtaken by a destructive, oozing swamp. The surface of everything looks corroded and eaten into.

Bird-like creatures stand guard outside the lonely ruins. Nightmarish images of strange creatures and parts of human beings are coming out of the paintwork.

There is a form near the middle of the painting which looks like the skull of an ox. This creature stretches out its forelegs which are armoured and made of metal. The ox or bull sometimes appears in art as a symbol of man's more primitive instincts.

Form

Structures which look like the ruined remains of buildings are covered with lifeless, decaying plantlife. Strange rocky shapes poke through the frozen swampland.

The colours Ernst has used are dark greens and muddy browns. None of them suggest fresh, new life but remind you of old and rotting vegetation.

The gloomy landscape stands out against the blue sky. The bright, natural-looking sky contrasts with the sickening heaps of twisted matter below.

When you look closely you begin to make out parts of human beings and other creatures trapped inside the encrusted rocky shapes.

Process

Ernst used the technique called *decalcomania* to create the effects in this painting.

Decalcomania involved spreading paint onto the canvas and then pressing a sheet of glass or paper into it. When these were removed some of the sticky surface of paint came off with them. This left behind a rich texture in the paint which made it appear furry, uneven and eaten into.

Ernst completed his paintings by drawing and painting over the top of this spontaneously created texture. When he let his mind wander over the rich painted surface he was able to give form to some of the strange images in his *unconscious* world.

Mood

Ernst has created an unnatural and ugly landscape. It creates a horrifying and sickening feeling in the viewer.

The dark greens and browns create a gloomy feeling. Everything is frozen at a point when it is decomposing. The shape of things is unclear and their surfaces are broken down.

Vox Angelica, 1943, by Max Ernst

Ideas:

- Make up a design using rectangles of different sizes. Draw objects in each section and express ideas which are important to you.

- Make a three-dimensional structure out of wood or other materials which has several sections in it. Then collect together objects, pictures, photos and other things that remind you of your own ideas or experiences and display them in your structure.

Background

Vox Angelica is a large painting, 152 cm × 203 cm, and its scale and structure are like a *medieval* altar-piece. Ernst was 52 years old when he painted this work and it is made up of 52 different sections. It is a record of many of the ideas and techniques of his painting career.

It was finished in the summer of 1943 when Ernst was staying in Arizona with another Surrealist artist called **Dorothea Tanning**, who became his wife in 1946. By this time he had been in America for two years and he used this holiday as a chance to assess what he had achieved in painting as well as starting to experiment with new ways of working.

The new direction his work was to take after this period can be seen in his painting called **Design in Nature** of 1947. This was created using a combination of precise geometry and shapes randomly produced by his new drip technique. By 1947, Europe had just survived the horrors of World War II and Ernst was trying to give his work a more hopeful tone. Unlike Ernst's earlier paintings of dark forests and petrified landscapes this work has a feeling of natural light and is painted in joyful, bright colours.

dynamic – full of moment, spirited, powerful.

randomly – something done randomly means that the outcome of the action is left to chance, for example, tossing a coin.

Content

This large piece of work is divided up into 52 paintings on rectangles of different sizes. Each section has a narrow frame around it and the scenes in them can be put into three groups.

The first group recalls earlier paintings of dark forests and shattered, dying landscapes. These sections are produced using the *decalcomania* and *grattage* techniques (see section on Process). The space within them is tight and restricted.

The second group has brighter and more colourful landscapes. They have blue skies and green fields and have a more spacious, open feeling.

The third group shows the tools used to produce art of a more calculated and geometric kind. Amongst these are rulers, set squares, *callipers* and other tools for measuring. These sections point the way to Ernst's experiments with a new way of working.

Form

Not only did Ernst develop new techniques in using paint but he also found new ways of using art from the past. **Vox Angelica** is built up on the lines of a medieval altar-piece with 52 different sections put together in a tight framework.

The sections are filled with contrasting images and colours which all go to make up one exciting painting. Dark panels contrast with lighter panels. Gold and reddish brown sections work well alongside the sky blue areas. Restricted spaces contrast with open landscapes. The tools of geometry contrast with *randomly* created textures and surfaces.

Process

This painting includes the techniques of *frottage* (rubbing), *grattage* (scraping) and *decalcomania* (producing textures by randomly lifting paint off the surface of the canvas).

Ernst also shows his first experiments with a new technique of dripping paint randomly over the canvas.

In this method, Ernst tied an empty can, with a tiny hole drilled into the bottom of it, to a piece of string one or two metres long. He filled the can with paint and allowed it to swing backwards and forwards over a flat canvas. Ernst guided the can by movements of his hands, arms, shoulders and his whole body. Lines of paint trickled onto the canvas and created a network of *dynamic* lines.

It was this method which fascinated a younger group of American artists called Abstract Expressionists. Painters like Jackson Pollock developed drip painting into action painting and created pictures like **Alchemy**, 1947 (see page 45) by walking over large canvases swinging his arms to drip and splash the paint onto the surface.

Mood

This work has a feeling of balance about it. Ernst shows examples of both his old and new ways of working. The framework of 52 rectangles allows your eyes to move across the surface of the painting enjoying the rich variety of Ernst's techniques and ideas.

This is an optimistic painting which looks forward to a new period in Ernst's artistic career. At the same time it is a thoughtful piece of work in which Ernst sums up the things he has achieved in the past.

Glossary

abstract – in abstract art, the artist does not want to record just the appearance of things but wants to focus on particular qualities in their work. For example, the power of colour was important to Expressionist artists and geometric structure was important to Cubist artists.

absurd – something which is out of place and doesn't make sense. It is usually impossible to explain.

ambiguity – an expression which has more than one meaning and this makes it unclear. Often completely different conclusions can be reached depending on which meaning is taken.

anagram – a word or phrase made by rearranging the letters of another word.

art movement – this is when a group of artists come together to explore a particular way or focus for the art they create, e.g. Impressionism, Expressionism, Cubism, Futurism, Surrealism, etc.

automatic/automatist – a way of doing things without thinking about it and without conscious control.

calliper – an instrument with two arms hinged at one end, used to measure curved sufaces.

collage – an artwork made from cutting up other materials and pictures and sticking them together to make a new design.

composition – the layout or formal design of a picture.

Communism/communist – name for movement of people who believe that the community should share all work and property according to wants and needs.

concrete irrationality – this was how Dalí described his aim of producing strange dream images from his unconscious mind which looked very real.

conscience/conscious – relating to the reasoning part of the mind we use when we are awake and are aware that we are thinking.

controversial – causing argument or difference of opinion.

decalcomania – a way of creating a texture in paint which can then be worked into to create different images. The paint is spread over the canvas and then a sheet of glass or paper is pressed into it and quickly pulled away to leave a sticky, furry paint surface.

distort/distortion – to twist or stretch something into a different shape, to deform it.

dynamic – full of moment, spirited, powerful.

enigmatic – mysterious, uncanny, hard to understand

Fascism/fascist – is an extreme nationalist movement. Fascists often believe that people's ideas and actions are a result of their race. They are opposed to the idea that people can solve their problems using reason. Fascist organisations usually have one strong leader.

foreboding – threatening.

foreground – the front of the picture.

Freud – Sigmund Freud (1856–1939) was the founder of psychoanalysis which was a method of helping people discover and work through hidden or unconscious ideas and desires. Freud believed these ideas were formed as a result of the experiences, thoughts and desires people had as infants and children.

frottage – a process of making rubbings from different surfaces such a floorboards, bark of trees, leaves, etc.

gestures – large, sweeping brushstrokes carried out in an unplanned way.

grattage – a technique of scraping away paint layers to show the canvas or other layers of dried paint beneath.

grotesque – when something looks very odd and unnatural, often ugly.

hallucination – an hallucination is something you see and believe to be real but is, in fact, only in your imagination.

image – any mental picture.

imagery – a picture or model of something.

incongruous – not belonging to the place it is in.

influence – something or someone which has affected the way an artist thinks or does something.

innovative – to be innovative is to make changes to the old way of doing things or to bring in new methods.

innovator – someone who makes changes.

intellectual – to be intellectual is to be concerned with producing ideas rather than making things.

manifesto – to explain what they were trying to do artists wrote down their aims and often published these and called them their manifesto.

Marxist – a Marxist is someone who believes in the ideas of Karl Marx (1818 1883). Marx said that society was divided into two main classes. These were the ruling class or capitalists who owned the machines needed to make things and the working class who had to work for them. Marxists thought the workers should have a revolution and establish a society without classes.

metaphysics – the study of the true reasons why things exist and why we think.

mysticism – an understanding of hidden truths about the world, usually of a religious kind.

myth – a very old story which tries to give an explanation for some of the things we know or believe in.

mythical – to do with the myths.

narcissism – an excessive love of oneself.

nuclear physics – a scientific body of knowledge about the smallest particles from which things are made. Nuclear physics made it possible to build a nuclear or atomic bomb of immense destructive power.

ominous – something that is strange and threatening and may be a warning of bad luck to come or an evil thing about to happen.

paranoia – a mental attitude where people distort and exaggerate their experiences.

perception – the way we directly understand the world through the senses such as seeing and touching, combined with thought.

perspective – viewpoint.

psychiatric – to do with the mind or mental disorders.

psychoanalyst – one who studies behaviours of the mind.

pun – a play on words that works by using a word which has two meanings.

randomly – something done randomly means that the outcome of the action is left to chance, for example, tossing a coin.

rational – using sense, reason or logic.

realistic – true-to-life. A description of something which people agree is close to its appearance. In the past, Western artists have been expected to follow the rules of perspective and shading if they wanted to produce a picture which would be described as realistic.

Republican – a Republican believes that a republic is the best form of government. A republic is a state without a king or queen which is ruled by the people, usually with elections.

representation – a way of showing how things look in an accurate and realistic way.

retrospective – a retrospective exhibition is one that looks back over an artists career and displays works completed over a long period.

revolutionary – rebelling against what was generally accepted.

socio-economic – socio-economic theories involve the idea that all parts of people's lives are affected by the way things are made and distributed.

spiritual – involving the inner, unworldly side of human understanding.

surreal – beyond the real, marvellous, fantastic.

Symbolist – the symbolist movement involved writers as well as artists. Symbolists were against realism in art and wanted to create pictures which were more imaginative and dreamlike.

symmetrical – when opposite halves of a figure, form, line or pattern are exactly the same.

technique – the way in which one creates a work of art or craft.

tradition/traditional – a tried and tested way of doing things which is often handed down from one generation to another.

transformation/transformed – changed from one form to another.

unambiguous – something which has one completely clear meaning.

unconscious – the part of our minds that we usually only become aware of in our dreams and not when we are awake and using our powers of reason.

unconventional – if you are unconventional you do not follow the rules that most people agree with.

Timeline

1891   Max Ernst is born on 2nd April

1898   René Magritte is born on 21st November

1900   Freud publishes *The Interpretation of Dreams*

1904   Salvador Dalí is born on 11th May

1914   World War I begins

1916   Dada begins at the Cabaret Voltaire in Zurich, Switzerland

1918   World War I ends

1919   André Breton publishes one of the first Surrealist writings called *Magnetic Fields*

1924   Breton publishes the first Surrealist Manifesto in Paris

1924   Breton publishes the Surrealist magazine *La Révolution Surrealiste*

1925   Ernst publishes a book of his frottages or rubbings called *Natural History*

1926   The Belgian Surrealist group is founded which includes Magritte

1928   Dalí and the director, Buñuel, produces the first Surrealist film called *Un Chien Andalou*

1928   Breton publishes *Surrealism and Painting*

1929   Breton publishes his second Surrealist Manifesto

1930   Ernst begins publishing a series of collage works. The most famous were called *Une Semaine de bonté* and *La Femme 100 têtes*

1931   The Surrealist magazine called *Minotaur* is published

1930   Max Ernst acts in another Surrealist film by the director Buñuel called *L'Age d'Or* or *The Golden Age*

1930   Magritte quarrels with Breton and leaves Paris for Belgium

1933   Breton and his other Surrealist colleagues are expelled from the Communist Party

1936   The Spanish Civil War begins

1938   International Surrealist exhibitions take place in Paris and Amsterdam

1939   Breton expels Dalí from the Surrealist group and Dalí goes to live in America with his wife Gala

1939   World War II begins

1941   Max Ernst flees from Europe and goes to America

1942   Dalí publishes his book called *The Secret Life of Salvador Dalí*

1945   World War II ends

1946   André Breton and the artist, Marcel Duchamp, organise the large International Surrealist Exhibition at the Galerie Maeght in Paris.

1949   Dalí returns from America to live in Spain

1950   Ernst returns to Europe from America

1962   Ernst has a retrospective exhibition at the Tate, London

1965   Magritte has a retrospective exhibition in The Museum of Modern Art in New York

1967   Magritte dies

1976   Ernst dies

1979   Dalí has a retrospective exhibition in Paris and London

1989   Dalí dies

Resource List

Books

Surrealism by Patrick WALDBERG, Thames and Hudson, 1978

Essential Surrealists by Tim MARTIN, Parragon, 1999

Magritte by Suzi GABLIK, Thames and Hudson, 1985

Magritte by A. M. HAMMACHER, Thames and Hudson, 1986

Magritte by Marcel PAQUET, Taschen, 2000

Max Ernst by Ulrich BISCHOFF, Taschen, 2003

Dalí by Gilles NERET, Taschen, 2002

Web sites

www.artchive.com

www.tate.org.uk/modern/default.htm

www.artnet.com

Photographic Credits